CHART HITS OF 2015-2016

FOR UKULELE

ISBN 978-1-4950-5822-6

HAL•LEONARD®
CORPORATION
7777 W. BLUEMOUND RD. P.O. BOX 13819 MILWAUKEE, WI 53213

Visit Hal Leonard Online at
www.halleonard.com

CONTENTS

Adventure of a Lifetime

Words and Music by Guy Berryman, Jon Buckland,
Chris Martin, Will Champion, Mikkel Eriksen and Tor Hermansen

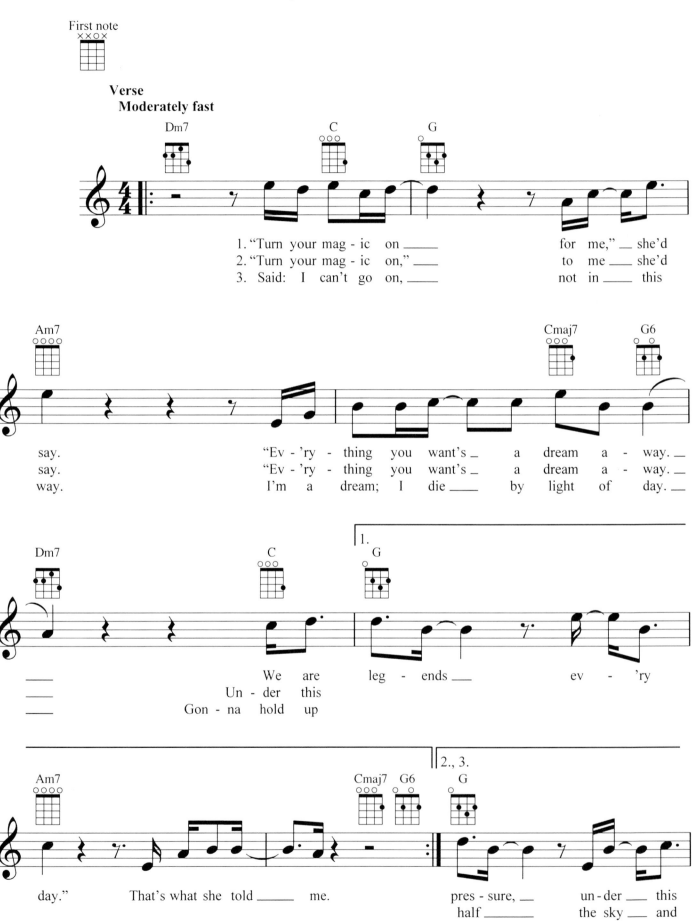

- monds tak - ing shape, _____ we are dia - monds tak - ing shape." _

Interlude

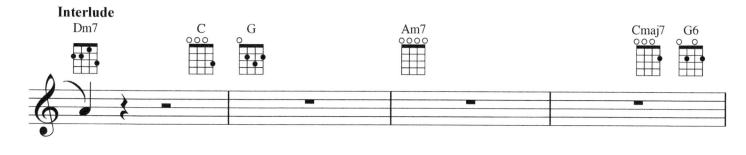

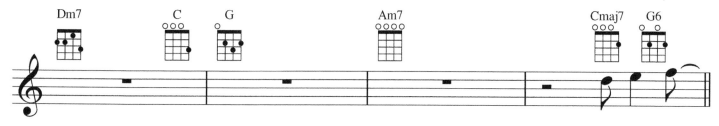

If we've on -

Bridge

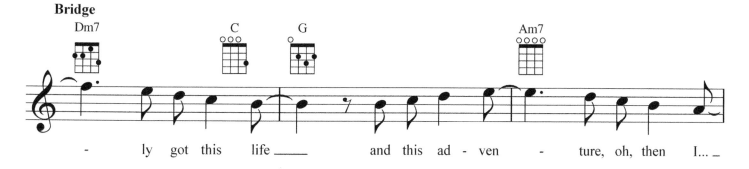

- ly got this life _____ and this ad - ven - ture, oh, then I... _

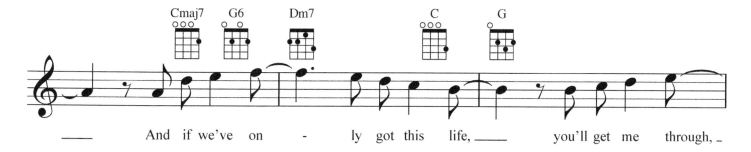

_____ And if we've on - ly got this life, _____ you'll get me through, _

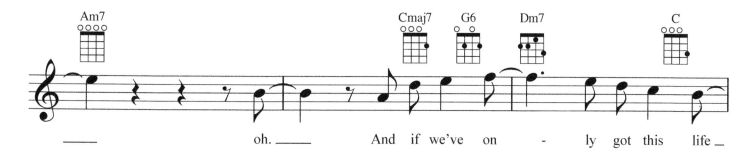

_____ oh. _____ And if we've on - ly got this life _

and this ad - ven - ture, oh, then I ____

____ wan - na share it with you, with you, with

you. ____ Sing it, oh, ____ sing, yeah. Woo -

Outro

hoo. (Woo - hoo.) Woo - hoo. (Woo - hoo.) Woo - hoo. ____ (Woo - hoo.) ____ Woo -

hoo. ____ (Woo - hoo.) ____ Woo - hoo. (Woo - hoo.) Woo -

hoo. (Woo - hoo.) Woo - hoo. ____ (Woo - hoo.) ____ Woo - hoo. ____ (Woo - hoo.) ____

Let It Go

Words and Music by James Bay and Paul Barry

First note

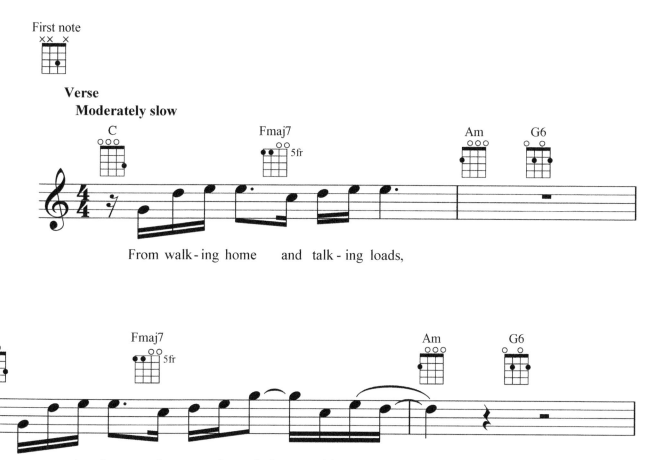

Verse
Moderately slow

From walk-ing home   and talk-ing loads,

to see-ing shows   in eve-ning clothes _ with you. _____

From nerv-ous touch   and get-ting drunk,

to stay-ing up   and wak-ing up _____ with you. _____   But now we're

you _____ and I'll ___ be me? ___ And I'll _____ be me. ___

2. From throw-ing clothes a-cross the floor,

to teeth and claws, and slam-ming doors ___ at you. _____

If this is all we're liv-ing for, ___ why are we

do-ing it, do-ing it, do - ing it an-y-more? I used to

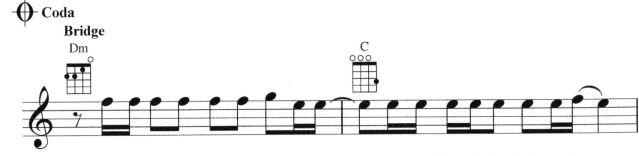

Coda

Bridge

Tryin' to fit your hand in-side of mine ___ when we know it just don't be-long. __

There's no force on earth ___ could make it feel right, ___ no. ___ Whoa. ___

Tryin' to push this prob-lem up the hill ___ when it's just too heav-y to hold. __

I think now's the time ___ to let ___ it slide. ___ So, come on, let it

Chorus

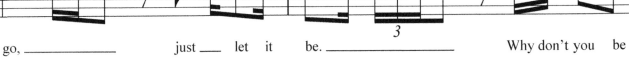

go, ___ just ___ let it be. ___ Why don't you be

you ___ and I'll ___ be me? ___ Ev-'ry-thing that's

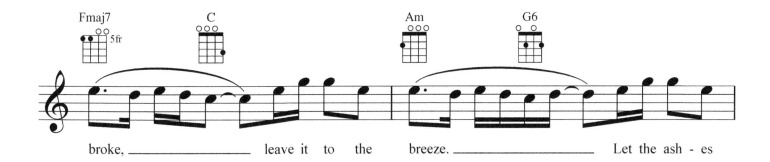

broke, _____ leave it to the breeze. _____ Let the ash - es

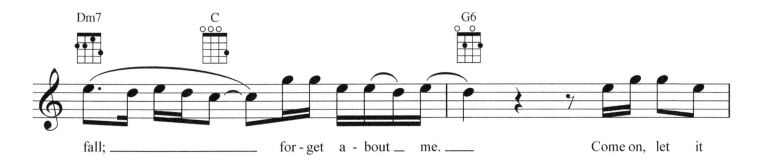

fall; _____ for - get a - bout __ me. ___ Come on, let it

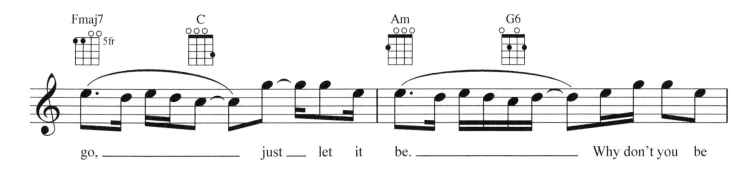

go, _____ just __ let it be. _____ Why don't you be

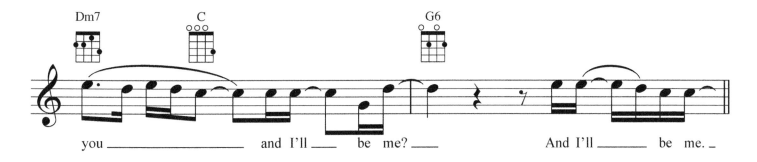

you _____ and I'll __ be me? ___ And I'll _____ be me. _

Outro

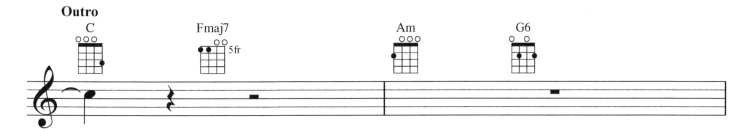

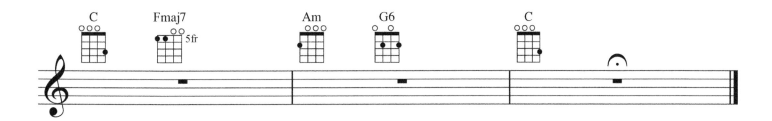

Budapest

Words and Music by George Barnett and Joel Pott

First note

Verse
Moderately fast

1. My house in Bu - da - pest; my, ___ my hid - den treas - ure chest; ___

gold - en grand pi - an - o; ___ my beau - ti - ful cas - til - lo: you, ooh, ___

you, ooh, ___ I'd leave it all.

Verse

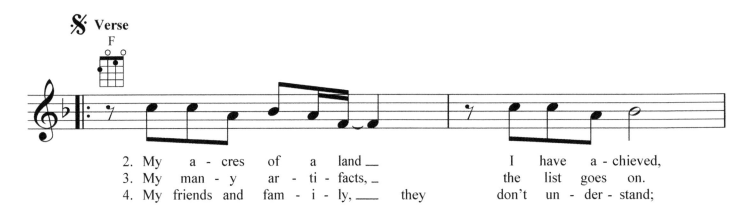

2. My a - cres of a land ___   I have a - chieved,
3. My man - y ar - ti - facts, ___   the list goes on.
4. My friends and fam - i - ly, ___ they don't un - der - stand;

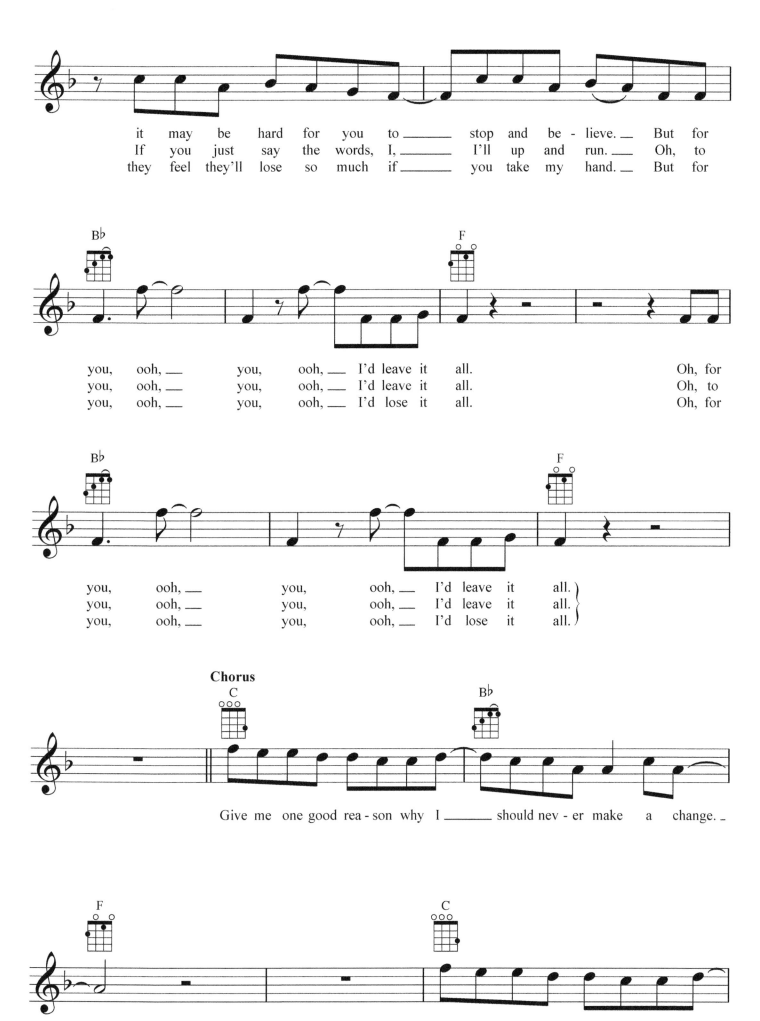

it may be hard for you to _____ stop and be - lieve. __ But for
If you just say the words, I, _____ I'll up and run. __ Oh, to
they feel they'll lose so much if _____ you take my hand. __ But for

Bb

F

you, ooh, __ you, ooh, __ I'd leave it all. Oh, for
you, ooh, __ you, ooh, __ I'd leave it all. Oh, to
you, ooh, __ you, ooh, __ I'd lose it all. Oh, for

Bb

F

you, ooh, __ you, ooh, __ I'd leave it all.
you, ooh, __ you, ooh, __ I'd leave it all.
you, ooh, __ you, ooh, __ I'd lose it all.

Chorus

C

Bb

Give me one good rea - son why I _____ should nev - er make a change. __

F

C

_____ Ba - by, if you hold me then all __

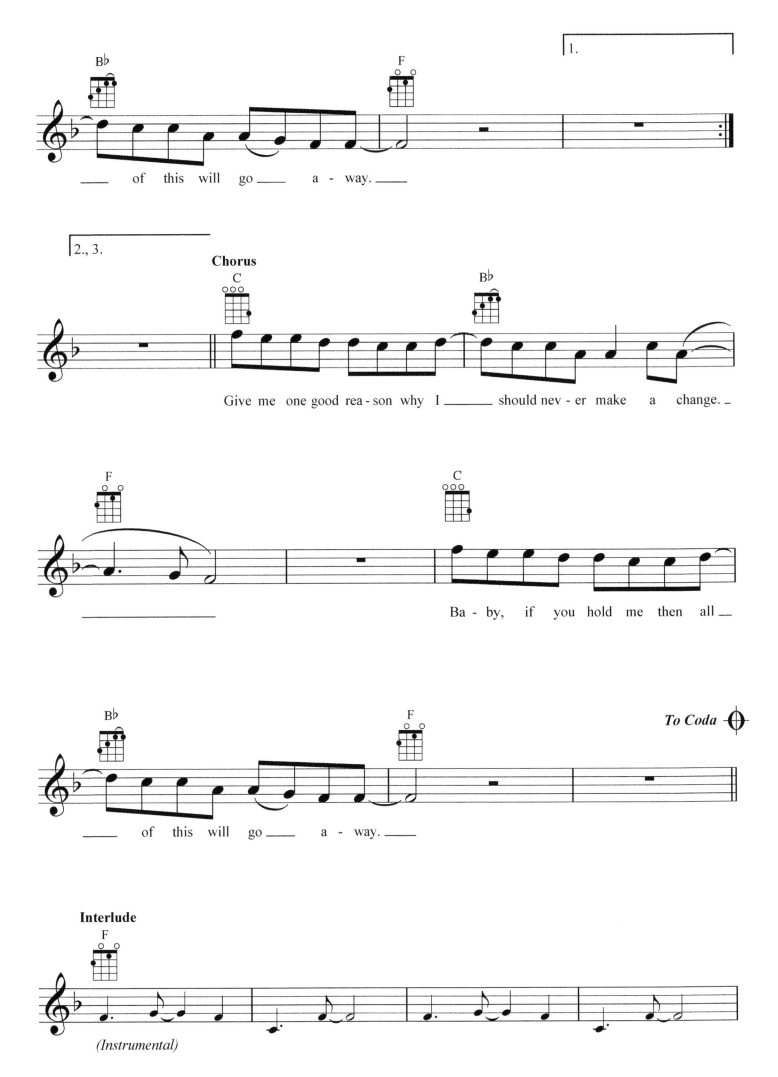

_of this will go ___ a - way. ___

Give me one good rea - son why I ___ should nev - er make a change. _

___

Ba - by, if you hold me then all _

_of this will go ___ a - way. ___

Interlude

(Instrumental)

Outro-Verse

Coda

My house in Bu - da - pest; my, ___ my hid - den treas - ure chest; ___

gold - en grand pi - an - o; _____ my beau - ti - ful cas - til - lo: you, ooh, ___

you, ooh, ___ I'd leave it all. Oh, for

you, ooh, ___ you, ooh, ___ I'd leave it all.

Burning House

**Words and Music by Jeff Bhasker,
Tyler Sam Johnson and Camaron Ochs**

1. I had a dream a-bout a burn-in' house. ___
(2.) see you at a par-ty and you look the same. ___

You were stuck in-side; ___ I could-n't get you
I could take you back, ___ but ___ peo-ple don't

out. ___
ev-er change. ___

I laid be-side ___ you and
Wish that we ___ could go

pulled you close. ___
back in time. ___

And the
I'd ___

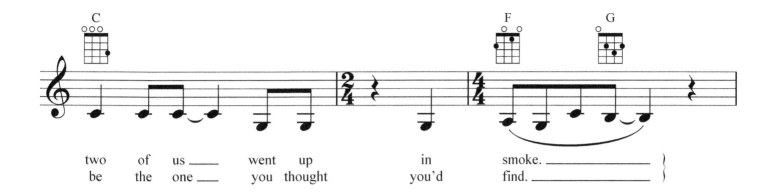

two   of   us ___   went   up   in   smoke. _____)
be   the   one ___   you   thought   you'd   find. _____)

Pre-Chorus

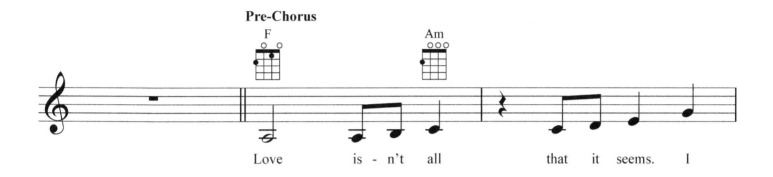

Love   is - n't   all   that   it   seems.   I

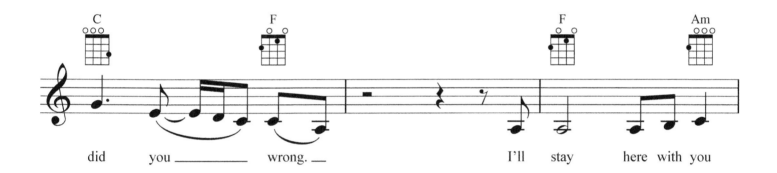

did   you _____   wrong. ___   I'll   stay   here   with   you

un - til   this   dream   is ___ gone.   I've   been

𝄋 **Chorus**

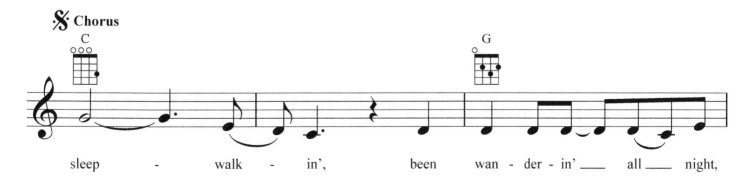

sleep - walk - in',   been   wan - der - in' ___ all ___ night,

tryin' to take ____ what's lost ___ and broke ___ and make __ it right.

I've been sleep - walk - in'

too close to the fire. _____ But it's the on - ly place ___ that I ___

____ can hold ___ you tight

in this

To Coda

1.

2.

burn - in' house. _____

2. I _____

The

Let chord ring.

Can't Feel My Face

**Words and Music by Abel Tesfaye, Max Martin,
Savan Kotecha, Peter Svensson and Ali Payami**

Pre-Chorus

She told me,"Don't wor - ry a - bout ___ it." She told me,"Don't

wor - ry no more." ___ We both know we can't ___ go with - out ___

___ it. She told me,"You'll nev - er be a - lone." Oh, oh, ooh.

Chorus

I can't feel my face when I'm with you, but I love ___ it, but I love _

___ it. Oh. ___ I can't feel my face when I'm with you, but I love _

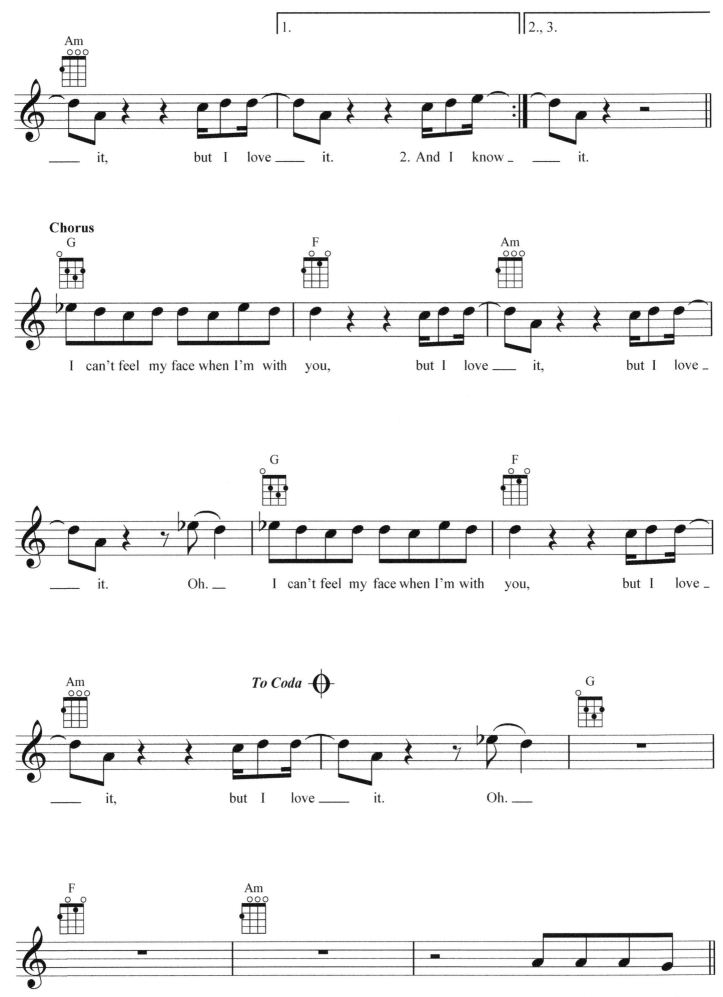

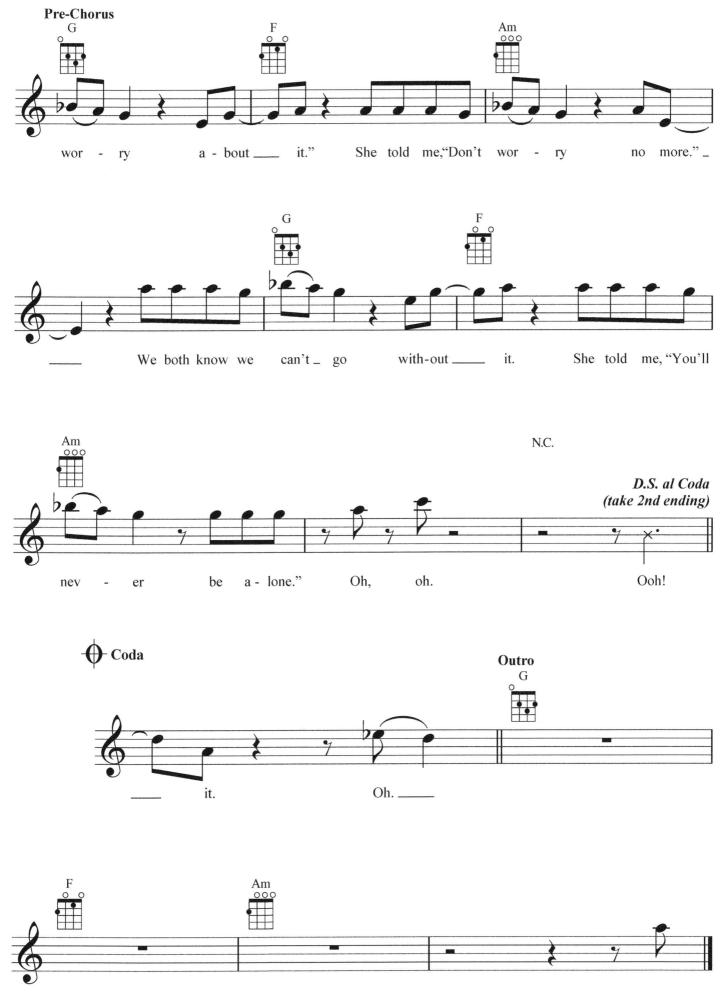

Ex's & Oh's

Words and Music by Tanner Schneider and Dave Bassett

I found me a bet-ter lov-er in the U. K., ____ hey, hey, ____
hearts ____ keep ____ break-ing and the heads just ____ roll. ____ You know ____

B7   Em
____ un - til I made my get - a - way.
____ that's how the sto - ry ____ goes. ____

𝄋 Pre-Chorus

N.C.

One, two, three, they gon - na run back to me, { (1., 2.) 'cause
                                                { (D.S.)

I'm the best ba - by that they nev - er got - ta keep.
climb - in' o - ver moun - tains and ____ sail - in' o - ver seas.

One, two, three, they gon - na run back to me. They al-ways wan - na come, but they

_____ me   like   gho - o - osts.   They   want _____   me   to   make 'em

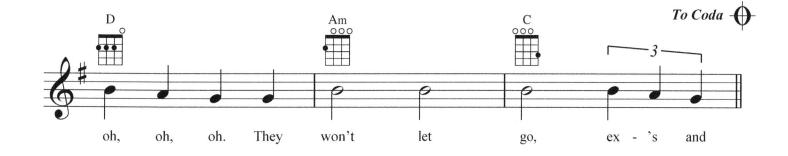

To Coda ⊕

oh,   oh,   oh.   They   won't   let   go,   ex - 's   and

Interlude

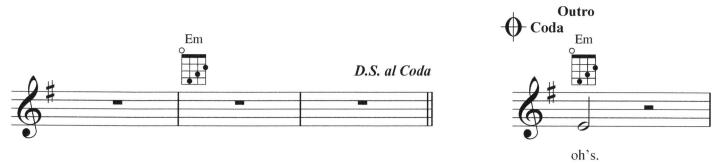

oh's.

Outro
⊕ **Coda**

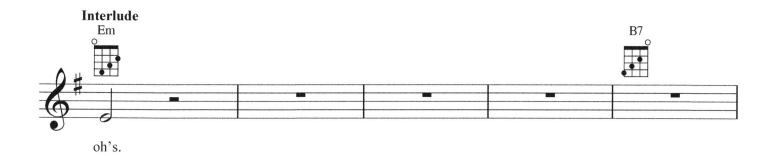

D.S. al Coda

oh's.

Hello

Words and Music by Adele Adkins and Greg Kurstin

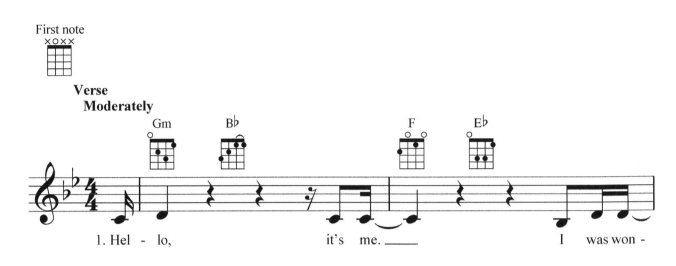

Verse
Moderately

1. Hel - lo, it's me. ___ I was won -

- der-ing ___ if, af - ter all ___ these years, ___ you'd like ___ to meet ___ to go o -

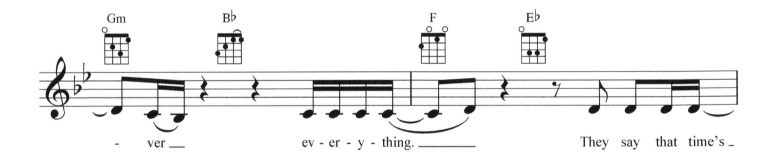

- ver ___ ev - er - y - thing. ___ They say that time's

___ sup-posed ___ to heal ___ ya, ___ but I ain't done much ___ heal - ing. 2. Hel -

Verse

Gm   B♭   F   E♭

lo,   can you hear ___ me?   I'm in Cal -
(3.) lo,   how are ___ you?   It's so

Gm   B♭   F   E♭

- i-for - nia, dream - ing a - bout who ___ we used ___ to be ___ when we were young -
typ - i-cal ___ of me ___ to talk ___ a - bout ___ my-self; ___ I'm sor - ry. I hope ___

Gm   B♭   F   E♭

- er ___   and free. _____ I've for - got -
___ that you're well. ___ Did you ev -

Gm   B♭   F   E♭

- ten how ___ it felt ___ be-fore ___ the world ___ fell at ___ our feet. ___ There's such a
- er make ___ it ___ out ___ of that town where noth - ing ev - er hap - pened? It's no

Pre-Chorus

Gm   F   Dm   E♭

dif - f'rence ___   be - tween ___ us, _____ and a
se - cret ___   that the both of us _____ are

31

Chorus

mil - li - on ____ miles. _____

run - ning out ___ of time. _____ So:⎫ Hel - lo from the oth - er side. _

_____ I must have called a thou - sand times _____ to tell you ___

___ I'm sor - ry for ev - 'ry - thing that I've done, _ but when I call ___

___ you nev - er seem to be home. ____ Hel - lo from the out - side. __

_____ At least I can say that I've tried ___

_____ to tell you _____ I'm sor - ry for

break-ing your heart. __ But it don't mat - ter: it clear - ly does-n't

1.

tear you a - part __ an - y - more. __   3. Hel -

2.   **Interlude**

tear you a - part __ an - y - more. __   *(Vocal ad lib.)*

D.S. al Coda

Coda

tear you a - part __ an - y - more. __

Like I'm Gonna Lose You

**Words and Music by Caitlyn Elizabeth Smith,
Justin Weaver and Meghan Trainor**

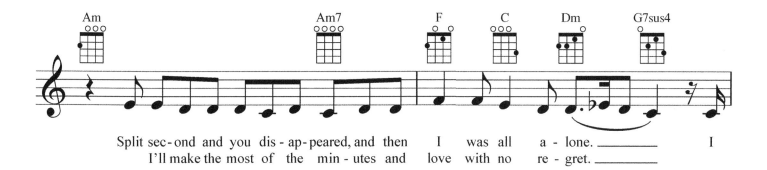

Split sec-ond and you dis-ap-peared, and then   I   was all   a - lone. _____   I
I'll make the most of the min - utes and   love with no   re - gret. _____

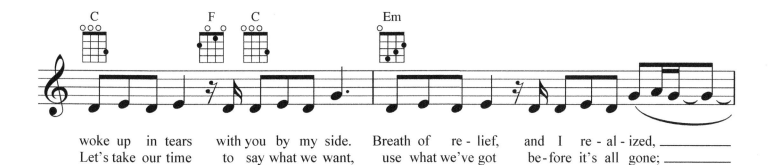

woke up   in tears   with you by my side.   Breath of   re - lief,   and I   re - al - ized, _____
Let's take our time   to   say what we want,   use what we've got   be - fore it's all gone; _____

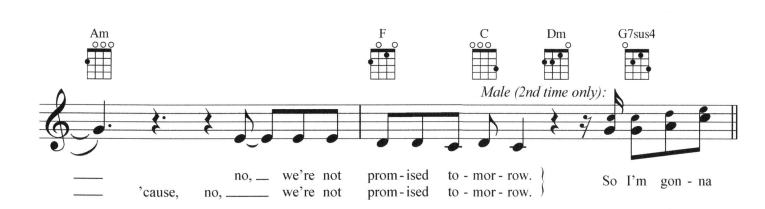

Male (2nd time only):

_____   no, __ we're not   prom - ised   to - mor - row. ⎫   So I'm gon - na
_____   'cause, no, _____ we're not   prom - ised   to - mor - row. ⎭

Chorus

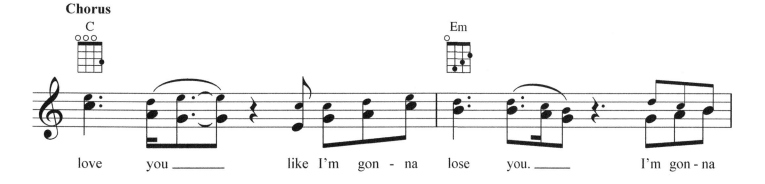

love   you _____   like I'm gon - na   lose   you. _____   I'm gon - na

Love Yourself

Words and Music by Justin Bieber, Benjamin Levin and Ed Sheeran

First note

Verse

Moderately

1. For all the times ____ that you rained ___ on my ___ pa - rade   and all the clubs ___
(2.) ____ me that you hat - ed ____ my friends,   the on - ly prob -

____ you   get   in   us - ing   my   name. ____   You think you   broke ___
- lem   was   with   you   and   not   them. ____   And ev - 'ry   time ___

____ my   heart;   oh,   girl,   for   good - ness' ____   sake.   You think I'm   cry -
____ you   told   me   my   o - pin - ion   was   wrong   and   tried   to   make ___

- ing   on   my   own;   well,   I   ain't. ____   And I   did - n't   wan - na
____ me   for - get   where   I   came   from. ____

Pre-Chorus 1

write a song ___ 'cause I did-n't want an-y-one think-ing I still care. I

don't, but you still hit my phone up. And, ba-by, I'll be

mov-ing on, ___ and I think it should be some-thing I don't wan-na

hold back. May-be you should know that my ma-ma don't

Pre-Chorus 2

like ___ you, and she likes ev-er-y-one. ___ And I ___ nev-er

like ___ to ad-mit that I ___ was wrong. ___ And I've been so

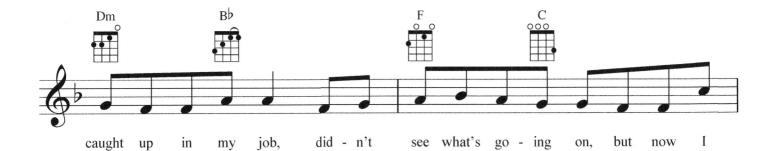

caught up in my job, did-n't see what's go-ing on, but now I

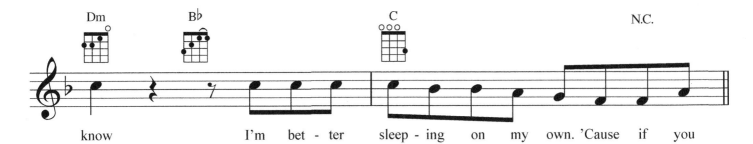

know I'm bet-ter sleep-ing on my own. 'Cause if you

Chorus

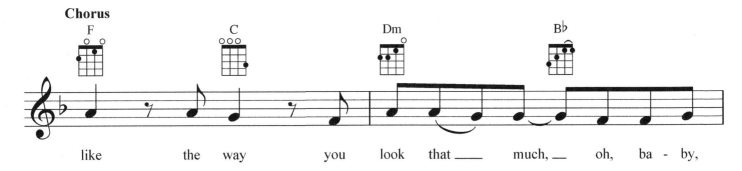

like the way you look that ___ much, ___ oh, ba - by,

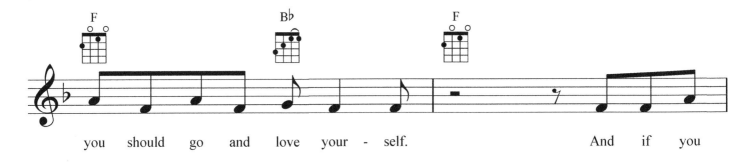

you should go and love your - self. And if you

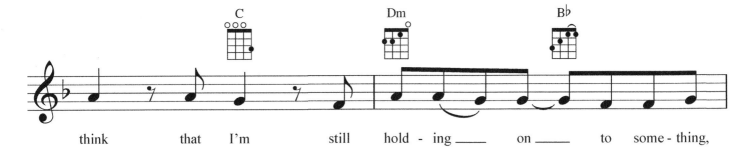

think that I'm still hold - ing ___ on ___ to some - thing,

you should go and love your - self. 2. But when you told ___

Outro-Chorus

42

Renegades

Words and Music by Alexander Junior Grant, Adam Levin,
Casey Harris, Noah Feldshuh and Sam Harris

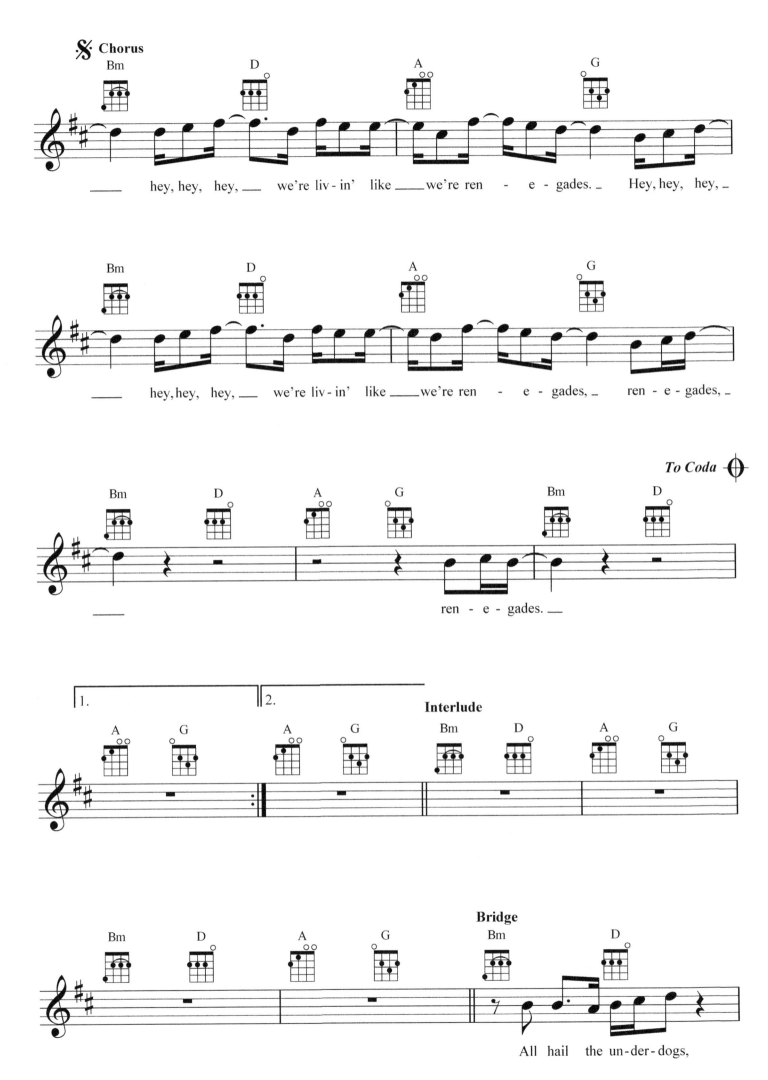

all hail the new kids,   all hail the out-laws,   Spiel-bergs and Ku-bricks.

It's our time   to make a move,   it's our time   to make a-mends.

D.S. al Coda

It's our time   to break the rules.   Let's be-gin. ___ And I say hey,___

Coda   Outro

1., 2.   3.

Perfect

Words and Music by Harry Styles, Louis Tomlinson, John Henry Ryan,
Jesse Shatkin, Maureen McDonald, Jacob Hindlin and Julian Bunetta

like hav - ing se - cret lit - tle ren - dez - vous, ___ if you

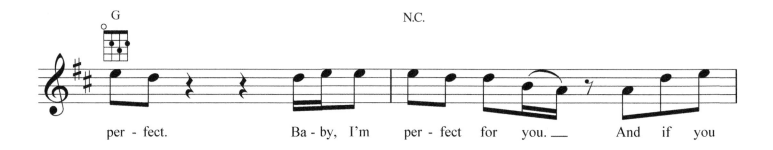

like to do the things you know that we should - n't do, ___ then, ba - by, I'm

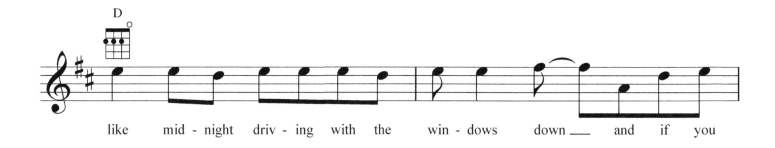

per - fect. Ba - by, I'm per - fect for you. ___ And if you

like mid - night driv - ing with the win - dows down ___ and if you

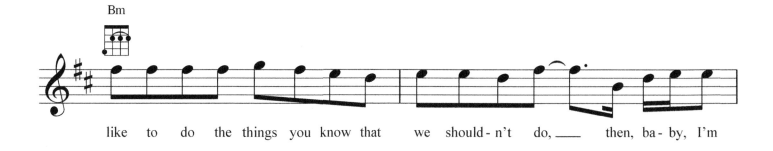

like go - ing plac - es we can't e - ven pro - nounce, ___ if you

like to do what - ev - er you've been dream - ing a - bout, ___ ba - by, you're

Stitches

Words and Music by Teddy Geiger,
Danny Parker and Daniel Kyriakides

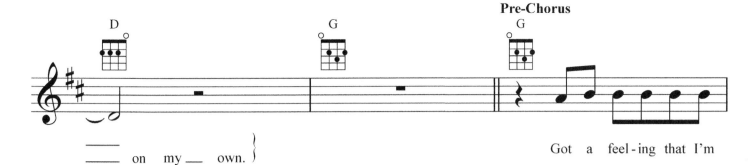

on my own. Got a feel-ing that I'm

go-in' un-der, but I know that I'll make it out a-live

if I quit call-ing you my lov-er and move on.

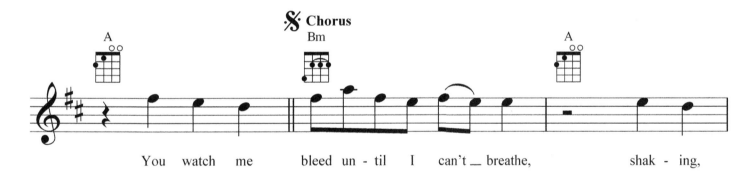

You watch me bleed un-til I can't breathe, shak-ing,

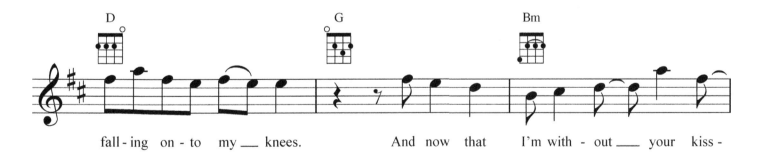

fall-ing on-to my knees. And now that I'm with-out your kiss-

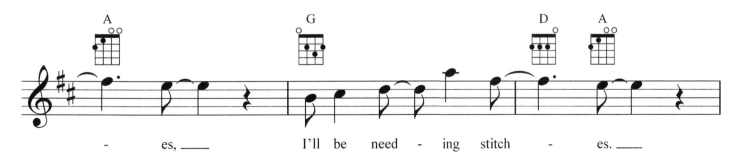

es, I'll be need-ing stitch-es.

Trip-ping o-ver my-self, ach-ing, beg-ging you to come _ help.

And now that I'm with-out ___ your kiss - es, ___

To Coda

Interlude

I'll be need - ing stitch - es. ___

Bridge

Nee - dle and the thread, got - ta

get you out of my head. Nee-dle and the thread, gon-na wind up dead.

Nee-dle and the thread, got-ta get you out of my head. Nee-dle and the thread, gon-na

wind up dead.   Nee - dle and the thread, got - ta   get you out of my head.

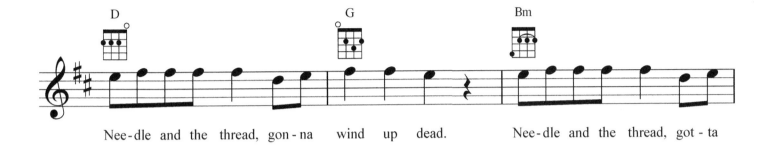

Nee - dle and the thread, gon - na   wind up dead.   Nee - dle and the thread, got - ta

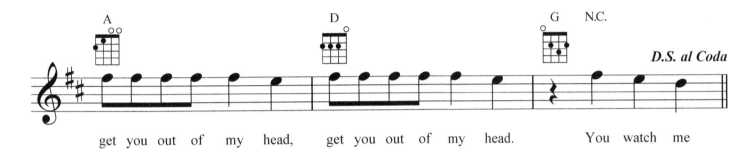

D.S. al Coda

get you out of my head,   get you out of my head.   You watch me

Coda   **Outro**

get you out of my head,   get you out of my head.   You watch me

- es. Now   that   I'm with - out ___ your kiss   - es, ___

I'll be need - ing stitch   - es. Now   that   I'm with - out ___ your kiss -

- es, ___   I'll be need - ing stitch   - es. ___

(Smooth As)
Tennessee Whiskey

Words and Music by Dean Dillon and Linda Hargrove

back _____ from be - in' _____ too far gone. _____ You're _ as

Chorus

smooth as Ten - nes - see whis - key, _____ you're _ as

sweet _____ as straw - ber - ry wine. __ You're as warm _

3   3   3   3   3

_____ as a glass _ of bran-

To Coda 2

dy, and, hon - ey, I ___ stay stoned ___ on your love ___ all ___ the

time.

2. I've looked for love ____ in all ____ the same old plac-

es.

Found the bot-tom of a bot-tle's al - ways dry. _____

_____ But when you poured _ out your heart, _ I did-n't waste

it, 'cause there's noth - in' _____ like your love _____ to get me high. _

D.S. al Coda 1

Coda 1

Interlude

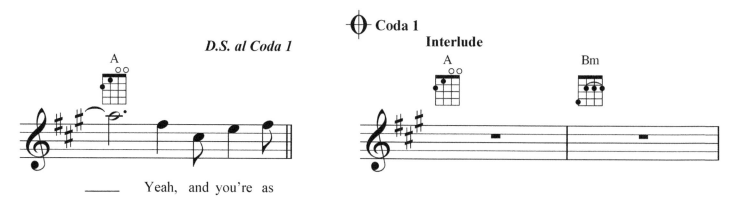

_____ Yeah, and you're as

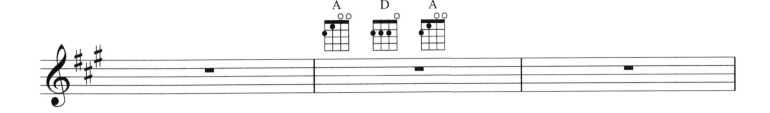

D.S. al Coda 2

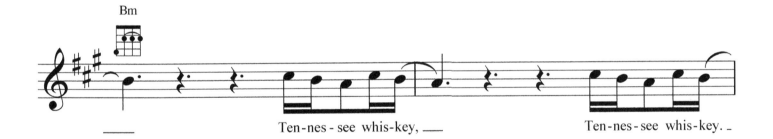

You're _ as

Coda 2   **Outro**

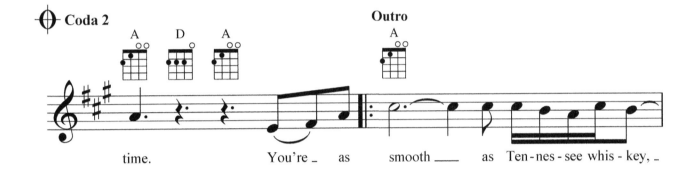

time.   You're _ as   smooth ___ as   Ten-nes-see whis-key, _

Ten-nes-see whis-key, ___   Ten-nes-see whis-key. _

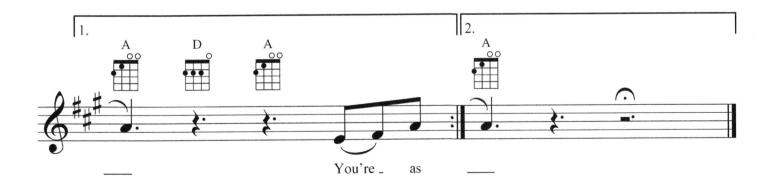

1.   2.

_   You're _ as   _

Tear in My Heart

Words and Music by Tyler Joseph

heart, I'm on fi - re. She's the tear in my ___ heart, take me high-

er than I've ev - er been. ___

er than I've ev - er been, ___

than I've ev - er been, ___

than I've ev - er been, ___

than I've ev - er been. ___ Oh oh ___ oh

oh. _____ Ooh ooh ___ ooh ooh ___ ooh. ___

You fell a - sleep in my car, I drove the whole time.

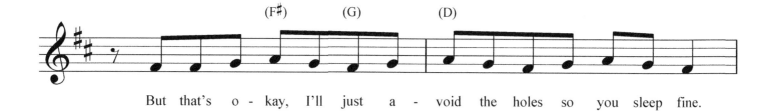

But that's o - kay, I'll just a - void the holes so you sleep fine.

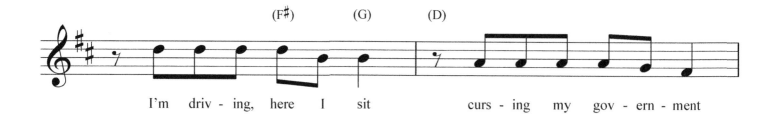

I'm driv - ing, here I sit curs - ing my gov - ern - ment

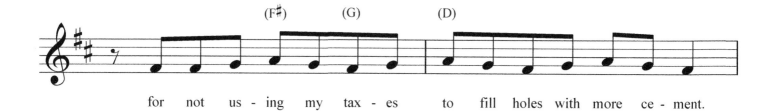

for not us - ing my tax - es to fill holes with more ce - ment.

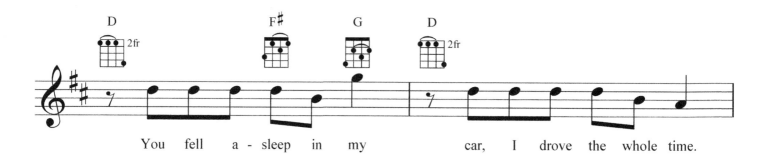

You fell a - sleep in my car, I drove the whole time.

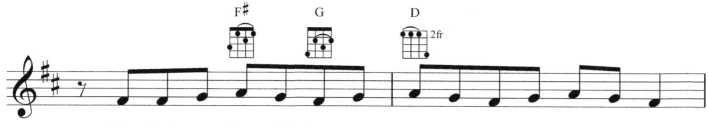

But that's o - kay, I'll just a - void the holes so you sleep fine.

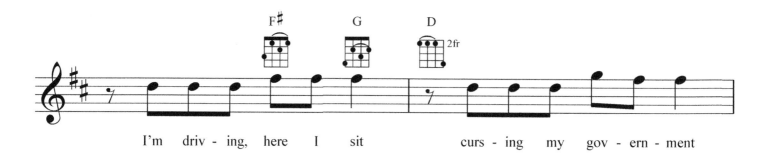

I'm driv - ing, here I sit curs - ing my gov - ern - ment

for not us-ing my tax-es to fill holes with more ce-ment.

Verse
Straight 8ths

Let chord ring.

3. Some-times you got-ta bleed to know, oh, ___ oh,

that you're a-live and have a soul - oul - oul. But it takes some-one to come a-

Chorus

round to show you how. ___ She's the tear in my ___ heart, I'm a-live. ___

___ She's the tear in my ___ heart, I'm on fi-re. She's the tear in my ___

Outro-Chorus

heart, take me high-er than I've ev-er been. ___ My heart is my ar-

mor. She's the tear in my __ heart, she's a carv - er. She's a butch-er with a

smile, cut me far - ther than I've ev - er been, __

than I've ev - er been, _____ than I've ev - er been, __

oh, _____ than I've ev - er been. _ My heart is my ar -
*Let chord ring.

mor. She's the tear in my heart, she's a carv - er. She's a butch-er with a

Slower, with freedom

smile, cut me far - ther than I've ev - er been.

Hal•Leonard®
UKULELE
PLAY-ALONG

AUDIO ACCESS INCLUDED

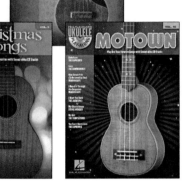

1. POP HITS
00701451 Book/CD Pack................$15.99

2. UKE CLASSICS
00701452 Book/CD Pack................$15.99

3. HAWAIIAN FAVORITES
00701453 Book/Online Audio $14.99

4. CHILDREN'S SONGS
00701454 Book/Online Audio $14.99

5. CHRISTMAS SONGS
00701696 Book/CD Pack................$12.99

6. LENNON & MCCARTNEY
00701723 Book/Online Audio $12.99

7. DISNEY FAVORITES
00701724 Book/Online Audio $12.99

8. CHART HITS
00701745 Book/CD Pack................$15.99

9. THE SOUND OF MUSIC
00701784 Book/CD Pack................$14.99

10. MOTOWN
00701964 Book/CD Pack................$12.99

11. CHRISTMAS STRUMMING
00702458 Book/Online Audio $12.99

12. BLUEGRASS FAVORITES
00702584 Book/CD Pack................$12.99

13. UKULELE SONGS
00702599 Book/CD Pack................$12.99

14. JOHNNY CASH
00702615 Book/CD Pack................$15.99

Prices, contents, and availability
subject to change without notice.

15. COUNTRY CLASSICS
00702834 Book/CD Pack................$12.99

16. STANDARDS
00702835 Book/CD Pack................$12.99

17. POP STANDARDS
00702836 Book/CD Pack................$12.99

18. IRISH SONGS
00703086 Book/Online Audio $12.99

19. BLUES STANDARDS
00703087 Book/CD Pack................$12.99

20. FOLK POP ROCK
00703088 Book/CD Pack................$12.99

21. HAWAIIAN CLASSICS
00703097 Book/CD Pack................$12.99

22. ISLAND SONGS
00703098 Book/CD Pack................$12.99

23. TAYLOR SWIFT – 2ND EDITION
00221966 Book/Online Audio $16.99

24. WINTER WONDERLAND
00101871 Book/CD Pack................$12.99

25. GREEN DAY
00110398 Book/CD Pack................$14.99

26. BOB MARLEY
00110399 Book/Online Audio $14.99

27. TIN PAN ALLEY
00116358 Book/CD Pack................$12.99

28. STEVIE WONDER
00116736 Book/CD Pack................$14.99

29. OVER THE RAINBOW & OTHER FAVORITES
00117076 Book/Online Audio $14.99

30. ACOUSTIC SONGS
00122336 Book/CD Pack................$14.99

31. JASON MRAZ
00124166 Book/CD Pack................$14.99

32. TOP DOWNLOADS
00127507 Book/CD Pack................$14.99

33. CLASSICAL THEMES
00127892 Book/Online Audio $14.99

34. CHRISTMAS HITS
00128602 Book/CD Pack................$14.99

35. SONGS FOR BEGINNERS
00129009 Book/Online Audio $14.99

36. ELVIS PRESLEY HAWAII
00138199 Book/Online Audio $14.99

37. LATIN
00141191 Book/Online Audio $14.99

38. JAZZ
00141192 Book/Online Audio $14.99

39. GYPSY JAZZ
00146559 Book/Online Audio $14.99

40. TODAY'S HITS
00160845 Book/Online Audio $14.99

HAL•LEONARD®

www.halleonard.com

Ride the Ukulele Wave!

The Beach Boys for Ukulele

This folio features 20 favorites, including: Barbara Ann • Be True to Your School • California Girls • Fun, Fun, Fun • God Only Knows • Good Vibrations • Help Me Rhonda • I Get Around • In My Room • Kokomo • Little Deuce Coupe • Sloop John B • Surfin' U.S.A. • Wouldn't It Be Nice • and more!

00701726 . . . . $14.99

Disney Songs for Ukulele

20 great Disney classics arranged for all uke players, including: Beauty and the Beast • Bibbidi-Bobbidi-Boo (The Magic Song) • Can You Feel the Love Tonight • Chim Chim Cher-ee • Heigh-Ho • It's a Small World • Some Day My Prince Will Come • We're All in This Together • When You Wish upon a Star • and more.

00701708 . . . . $14.99

Jack Johnson – Strum & Sing

Cherry Lane Music
Strum along with 41 Jack Johnson songs using this top-notch collection of chords and lyrics just for the uke! Includes: Better Together • Bubble Toes • Cocoon • Do You Remember • Flake • Fortunate Fool • Good People • Holes to Heaven • Taylor • Tomorrow Morning • and more.

02501702 . . . . $19.99

The Beatles for Ukulele

Ukulele players can strum, sing and pick along with 20 Beatles classics! Includes: All You Need Is Love • Eight Days a Week • Good Day Sunshine • Here, There and Everywhere • Let It Be • Love Me Do • Penny Lane • Yesterday • and more.

00700154 . . . . $16.99

First 50 Songs You Should Play on Ukulele

An amazing collection of 50 accessible, must-know favorites: Edelweiss • Hey, Soul Sister • I Walk the Line • I'm Yours • Imagine • Over the Rainbow • Peaceful Easy Feeling • The Rainbow Connection • Riptide • and many more.

00149250 . . . . $14.99

Elvis Presley for Ukulele

arr. Jim Beloff
20 classic hits from The King: All Shook Up • Blue Hawaii • Blue Suede Shoes • Can't Help Falling in Love • Don't • Heartbreak Hotel • Hound Dog • Jailhouse Rock • Love Me • Love Me Tender • Return to Sender • Suspicious Minds • Teddy Bear • and more.

00701004 . . . . $15.99

The Daily Ukulele

compiled and arranged by

Liz and Jim Beloff
Strum a different song everyday with easy arrangements of 365 of your favorite songs in one big songbook! Includes favorites by the Beatles, Beach Boys, and Bob Dylan, folk songs, pop songs, kids' songs, Christmas carols, and Broadway and Hollywood tunes, all with a spiral binding for ease of use.

00240356 . . . . $39.99

Folk Songs for Ukulele

A great collection to take along to the campfire! 60 folk songs, including: Amazing Grace • Buffalo Gals • Camptown Races • For He's a Jolly Good Fellow • Good Night Ladies • Home on the Range • I've Been Working on the Railroad • Kumbaya • My Bonnie Lies over the Ocean • On Top of Old Smoky • Scarborough Fair • Swing Low, Sweet Chariot • Take Me Out to the Ball Game • Yankee Doodle • and more.

00696068 . . . . $12.99

Jake Shimabukuro – Peace Love Ukulele

Deemed "the Hendrix of the ukulele," Hawaii native Jake Shimabukuro is a uke virtuoso. Our songbook features note-for-note transcriptions with ukulele tablature of Jake's masterful playing on all the CD tracks: Bohemian Rhapsody • Boy Meets Girl • Bring Your Adz • Hallelujah • Pianoforte 2010 • Variation on a Dance 2010 • and more, plus two bonus selections!

00702516 . . . . $19.99

The Daily Ukulele – Leap Year Edition

366 More Songs for Better Living

compiled and arranged by
Liz and Jim Beloff
An amazing second volume with 366 MORE songs for you to master each day of a leap year! Includes: Ain't No Sunshine • Calendar Girl • I Got You Babe • Lean on Me • Moondance • and many, many more.

00240681 . . . . $39.99

Hawaiian Songs for Ukulele

Over thirty songs from the state that made the ukulele famous, including: Beyond the Rainbow • Hanalei Moon • Ka-lu-a • Lovely Hula Girl • Mele Kalikimaka • One More Aloha • Sea Breeze • Tiny Bubbles • Waikiki • and more.

00696065 . . . . $10.99

Worship Songs for Ukulele

25 worship songs: Amazing Grace (My Chains are Gone) • Blessed Be Your Name • Enough • God of Wonders • Holy Is the Lord • How Great Is Our God • In Christ Alone • Love the Lord • Mighty to Save • Sing to the King • Step by Step • We Fall Down • and more.

00702546 . . . . $14.99

HAL•LEONARD®

Prices, contents, and availability subject to change.